Mystery history of a Medieval castle

Jim Pipe

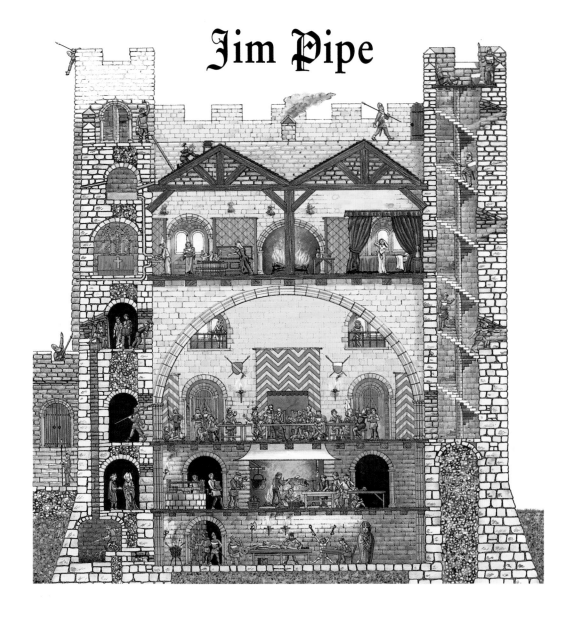

Copper Beech Books
Brookfield, Connecticut

© Aladdin Books Ltd 1996

Designed and produced by
Aladdin Books Ltd
28 Percy Street
London W1P 0LD

First published in
the United States in 1996 by
Copper Beech Books
an imprint of
The Millbrook Press
2 Old New Milford Road
Brookfield, Connecticut
06804

Editor
Jon Richards

Designed by
David West Children's Book
Design
Designer
Simon Morse
Illustrated by
Mike Bell, Richard Berridge –
Specs Art, Roger Hutchins
Additional illustrations by
David Burroughs
Rob Shone

Printed in Belgium

Library of Congress
Cataloging-in-Publication Data
Pipe, Jim, 1966-
   Medieval castle / by Jim Pipe;
illustrated by Dave Burroughs, Roger
Hutchins, Peter Berridge.
      p. cm. — (Mystery history)
   Includes index.
   Summary: Describes life in a castle
during the Middle Ages, covering home
life, feasts, jousting, sieges and more.
Includes games, puzzles, and mazes.
   ISBN 0-7613-0495-9 (lib. bdg.). —
ISBN 0-7613-0501-7 (hardcover)
   1. Castles—Juvenile literature.
2. Civilization, Medieval—Juvenile
literature. [1. Castles. 2. Civilization,
Medieval.] I. Burroughs, Dave, 1952- ill.
II. Hutchins, Roger, ill. III. Berridge,
Peter, ill. IV. Title. V. Series.
GT3550.P56 1996
940.1—dc20   96-12638 CIP AC

Contents

The Medieval Castle

To enter a medieval castle was to enter a world of loyalty, treachery, intrigue, and mystery. Within the thick castle walls lay secret passages, hidden corners where traitors whispered fiendish plots, and dungeons where prisoners were locked up and forgotten.

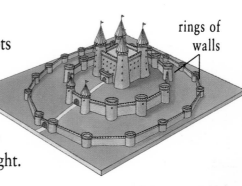

The castle in this book dates from around 1350 A.D., but the great age of castles began almost 400 years before. The first were built of wood, and stood on a mound called a motte (*above*). Below the motte was a walled area called a bailey.

By the 1100s, stone keeps had become the main castle stronghold. From the 1220s, the lord of the castle relied on rings of walls and towers, rather than the central keep (*left* and *below*), to protect him from his enemies.

motte

bailey

keep

rings of walls

The Mystery of History

Some medieval castles and manuscripts survive in pretty good shape – but they can only tell us part of the story. So as you read, try to imagine what life must have been like – who knows, your guess might be right. That's the real mystery of history!

Using Mystery History

You'll find that *Mystery History of a Medieval Castle* is packed with puzzles and mysteries for you to solve. But before you go any further, read the instructions below to get the most out of the book!

Hunt the Assassin

You'll see the assassin on many pages, on his mission to kill the Queen. His identity is hidden by a brown cloak and hood, but on page 29 a number of suspects have been rounded up. To help you figure out which of them is the assassin, six clues are given in the assassin boxes (the panels with a dagger in them). But to get the right clues you must answer the questions correctly – and that means reading the book carefully!

The Rook's Puzzles

The rook indicates a special puzzle that can be anything from a maze to a historical brainteaser. Certainly not for bird brains! Answers are in Ye Olde Answers.

True or False

Some spreads have a teasing True or False question with an answer (on page 29) that may surprise you!

Jester's Quest

Try to spot the items hidden on each spread, then guess if they belong in a medieval castle! For the answers see Ye Olde Answers.

History Mysteries

Dotted around the page are questions like: Q3 Is there any way to sneak into a castle? Take time to think about these before reading the answer in Ye Olde Answers.

Ye Olde Answers

Answers to Jester's Quest, the History Mysteries Q3, and the Rook's Puzzles are given in this bottom panel.

The Castle Game

At the back of the book are full answers to the Jester's Quest and True or False, plus a rogues' gallery of guilty-looking villains (one of whom is the assassin) and last, but not least, a great aerial view of the castle under siege that is also an exciting game (right)!

The Gatehouse

owering above the track that leads to the castle is the gatehouse. As the castle's only entrance, it has especially thick walls to make it harder for attackers to get in. There's a long line of knights, traders, and priests trying to enter. But the busybody sentries are on the look out for anyone suspicious (Can you spot anything?), so they are searching the carts and asking lots of tricky questions. Often the best way to get past quickly is to slip them a bribe. Perhaps a tasty pie or a silver coin will do!

As the castle is also protected by a moat, a deep ditch filled with water that circles the walls, everyone must cross a wooden drawbridge. This is raised at night or when danger threatens.

Q2 Does everyone live in a castle?

Drawbridge

◇ Jester's Quest
Can you spot the glass window, pipe, television, and hammer? Which don't belong in a medieval castle?

Q1 Who wants to live in a freezing castle?

Ye Olde Answers

Q1 Everyone! Castles may be cold, damp, and windy, but they do keep you safe from enemies and bandits. They also give you a base from which you can control the nearby countryside. And by the 1200s, castles were being built with comfortable rooms to live in and strong defenses.

Q2 No, only those who can afford it live in a castle. To build a castle is very expensive, so only rich nobles can pay for them, and only their knights can afford the rent for rooms there. Most servants, traders, and peasants live in villages that are not too far away.

Jester's Quest: The pipe and television don't belong. Full answers are on page 28.

Gatehouse

Portcullis

Storeroom

Dungeon

Hunt the Assassin

Choose your answer and use the clue it gives you to discover who the assassin is on page 29.

Early castles were built from:

a stone = Red hat
b wood = Brown hat
c sand = Iron helmet

Q3 Is there any way to sneak into a castle?

True or false?
A castle was
once built in a single night.

Q3 Not really! Many castles are built on high ground, making it very difficult to creep up without being seen. However, in 1204 some soldiers attacking Château Gaillard in France did manage to sneak into a castle – by climbing up the toilet shaft (see page 10)!

5

A Fabulous Feast

Now safe inside the castle, these guests can enjoy the highlight of the day – the banquet. A fanfare announces a procession of servants, who are bringing in the food on large dishes called messes. The lord and his special guests have silver plates, but most people are eating off a slice of stale bread which soaks up all the grease from the food.

It's a noisy but cheerful occasion, and everyone shares wine from their goblets and food from the messes with their neighbors.

Q1 What's the food like?

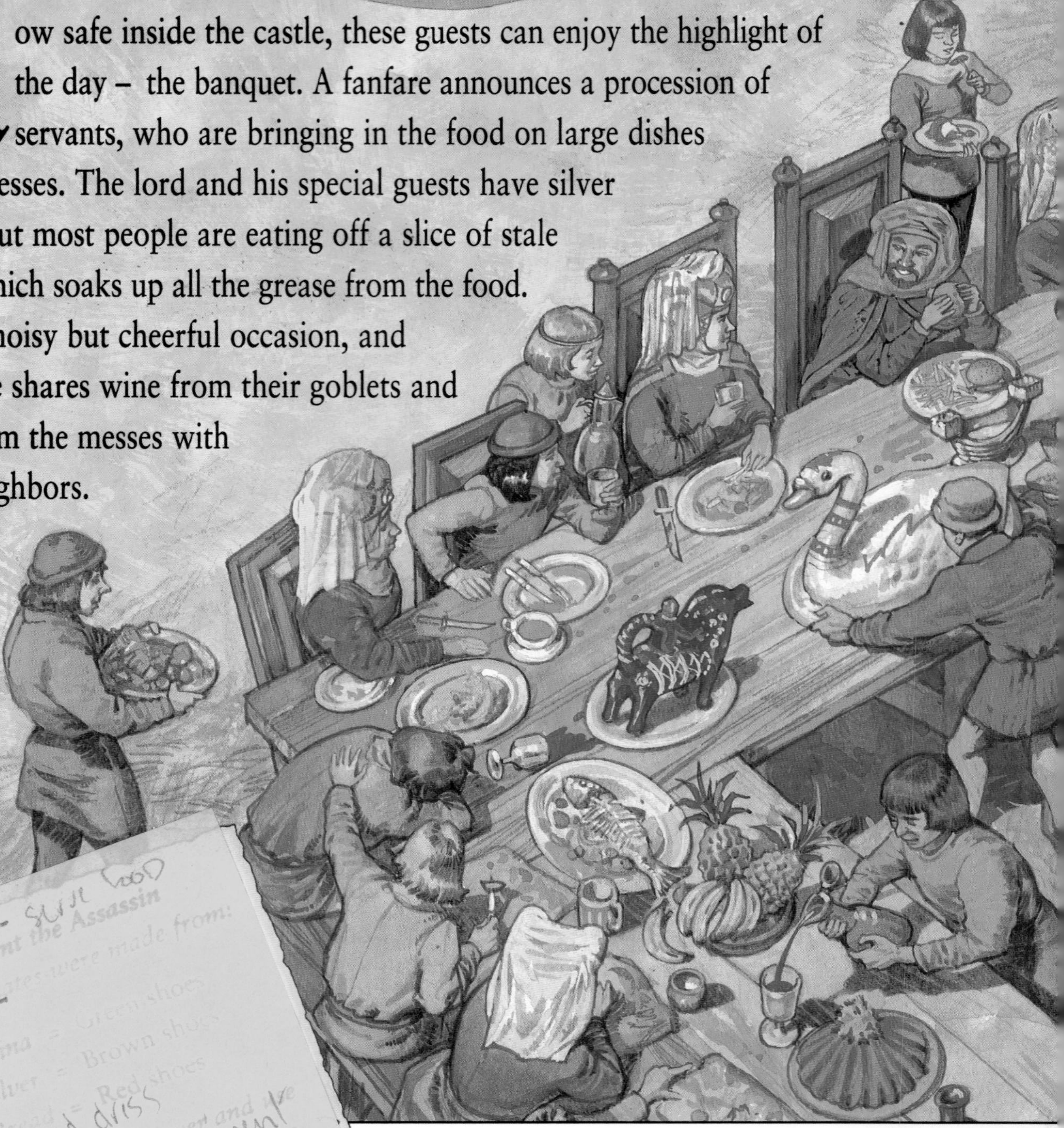

pages/squires – serve food
Queen/King –
Knights –
maiden – head dress
musician – entertainment
Jesters – entertainment

[illegible]wers

Q1 [illegible] the year, the food eaten in the castle is very basic – bread, [illegible] vegetables, and a little meat. But when the lord is home, the kitchen buzzes with activity.

Some of the food probably tastes very good – but without refrigerators it quickly goes bad. To prevent this, meat is preserved in salt, and vegetables are dried or pickled. Strong flavors are used to disguise bad food, so it is easy to poison. Everything nobles eat and drink is tasted first by a servant. However, French baron Robert the Giroie managed to swallow a poisoned apple his wife Adelaide had prepared for another man!

Q2 Is cleaning up easy after a medieval dinner?

Q3 Is that a live swan on the table?

Puzzling Manners

There have always been messy eaters (you probably know some), but even in medieval times there are rules about behavior at the table. Which of the following do you think *aren't* rules:

a Don't break wind or belch
b Don't leave any food on your plate
c Don't pick your teeth with a knife
d Don't spit on the table
e Don't drink too much wine

One thing you can be is very rough with your food. The lord and his family are treated to soft cheese, but the cheese eaten by everyone else is so tough that it has to be smashed into edible pieces with a hammer!

Jester's Quest
Can you spot the jelly, pineapples, tea, bananas, burger and fries, corn-on-the-cob, and beer. Which wouldn't be on a medieval table?

Q2 No. People do eat with their fingers and knives, so there are no forks and few spoons to clean, and the pieces of bread used as plates are given to the poor. But there is no dishwashing liquid, so dirty pans are cleaned with sand, soapy herbs like soapwort, and a lot of hard work!

Q3 No. It may look like a live swan, but in fact the cooks have simply plucked and roasted the bird, then stuck back on all the feathers for decoration. Medieval cooks also color food with bright vegetable dyes and sometimes even cover it in shavings of real gold!

Puzzling Manners
b & e. If you are rich enough to be at the feast, you leave food you don't want, and drink as much as you like!

Jester's Quest: Pineapples, bananas, tea, fries, and corn-on-the-cob. For the full answers, turn to page 28.

That's Entertainment

The eating is over and the jester and tumblers are entertaining the diners with jokes, rhymes, acrobatics, and juggling. Guests will later play games such as hoodman blind, when one person's head is covered and he or she has to chase after the other players. Troubadours are singing songs, telling epic tales of great champions and their bravery and lovers.

Dancing is also extremely popular and a drummer beats time to give the music a strong beat. In the old-style dances everyone holds hands in a ring or forms a chain, but couples also dance together in the very latest (14th-century!) dances.

Q1 Isn't castle life very boring without TV?

Jester

Jester's Quest
Can you spot the guitar, tennis ball, Walkman, and watch? Which don't belong in a medieval castle?

Ye Olde Answers

Q1 Not for the nobles! As well as enjoying the live entertainment of troubadours and acrobats, they spend many hours playing chess, checkers, backgammon, dice, and – from the 15th century onward – cards. Life is action-packed for the men, who spend their days hunting, taking part in tournaments, and training. Many women also hunt. They also play instruments and write songs at home.

Jester's Quest: None really belong! For the full reasons why, turn to page 28.

Q2 How are castles lit at night?

Tumblers

True or false?
Some troubadours acted as spies.

Time Puzzle

Knowing the exact time of day is not as important to medieval people as it is to city-dwellers in the 20th century. Clocks were developed in Europe in about 1200, but they were expensive and rare, so sundials (*above*) and candles were used. This candle (*right*) burns through a ring every 2 hours and was lit when the feast began. From the main picture, can you tell how long the fun has lasted?

Q3 Was a fool foolish?

Q2 In larger rooms and corridors, flaming torches light the way. In private rooms, wax candles are used. In older castles, fires are put in the middle of the great hall. The castle soon becomes very smoky and makes it even more difficult to see where you are going. Perfect for an assassin!

Q3 It is the fool's (jester's) job to make people laugh, which means a lot of fooling around. He wears a cap with bells hanging from it and carries a stick with a sheep's bladder attached (a slapstick). But the fool can also joke about and criticize his lord when others would never dare to.

Time Puzzle
The candle on the table is only showing four rings, so three of the original seven have melted away. As one ring equals two hours, then the answer is 3 x 2 = 6 hours. In fact, many banquets started at 10 in the morning and lasted into the night!

The Keep

Banquets are held in the great hall, which is usually at the heart of the castle in the keep, or great tower. Upstairs are the private rooms, known as solars, where the lord and his family live. Further up, on the battlements, is the lookout, nicknamed "Jim Crow," because of his high perch.

Below are the kitchens, though in many castles they are put in a separate building to protect the keep from spreading fire. And down in the darkest, dampest part of the castle are the dungeons, where prisoners lie rotting in chains...

Hunt the Assassin

The most common way to get out of the dungeons was to:

a Dig a tunnel = Brown hair
b Bribe a guard = Fair hair
c Ask very nicely = Black hair

Use your answer to uncover the assassin on page 29!

Jester's Quest
Can you spot the mummy's coffin, torture rack, plumbing, and telephone? Which don't belong in a medieval castle?

Lady's Bedroom

Q1 Why do stairs wind clockwise?

True or False?
Castles had booby traps.

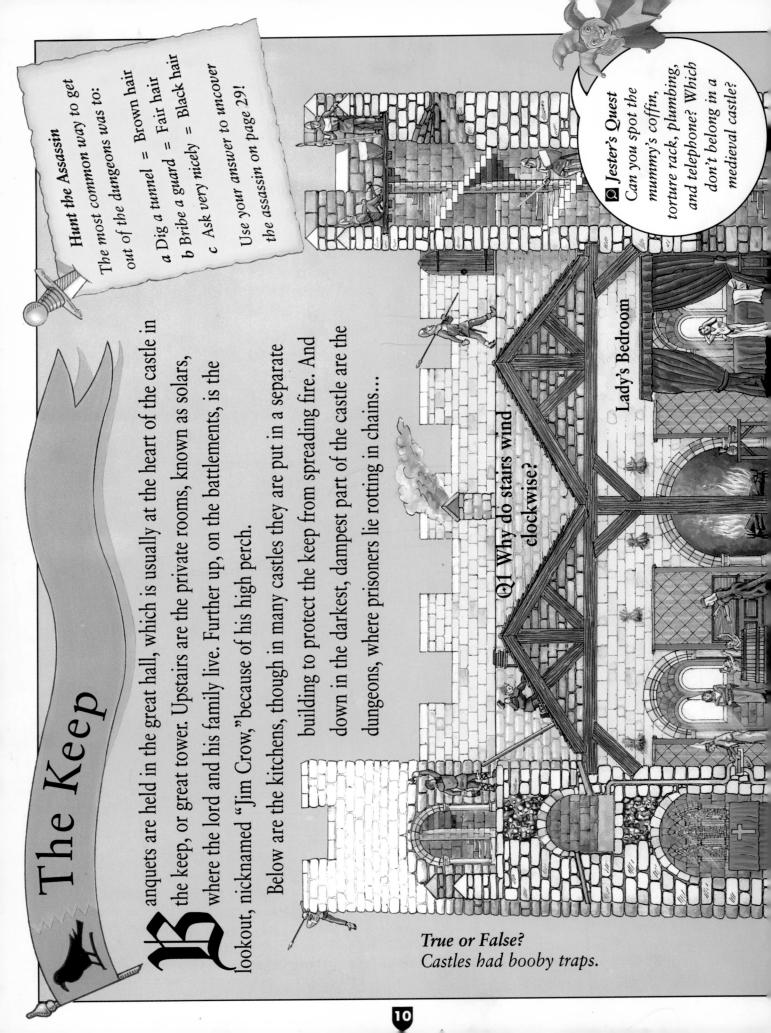

Q2 Who is put in the dungeons and tortured?

Great Hall

Kitchen

Dungeon

Smells Odd?

1 In what room would you find:
- Clothes being stored
- Sweet-smelling herbs on the floor
- Strips of linen?

2 King John of England only bathed once a month. This was partly because medieval people weren't so fussy about keeping themselves clean. Can you think of another reason why he had so few baths?

Jester Quest: The telephone and mummy's coffin don't belong. For the full reasons why, turn to page 28.

Smells Odd:

1 In the toilet, called a garderobe because people hang clothes there as the smell stops moths from eating them.

2 Because it costs almost a week's wages per bath – for the wood to heat up the water, for the bath oils, and for the soap!

Ye Olde Answers

Q1 Most knights hold their sword in their right hand, so stairs that spiral clockwise give the advantage to defenders, who would naturally have much more space to swing their sword.

Q2 Most prisoners are captured nobles being held until the ransom money arrives – criminals and ordinary soldiers are simply executed. Prisoners must also pay for their own food and the most common form of getting out is by bribing the jailers! Few people are actually tortured, though some are put in tiny rooms and simply forgotten about!

Castle Life

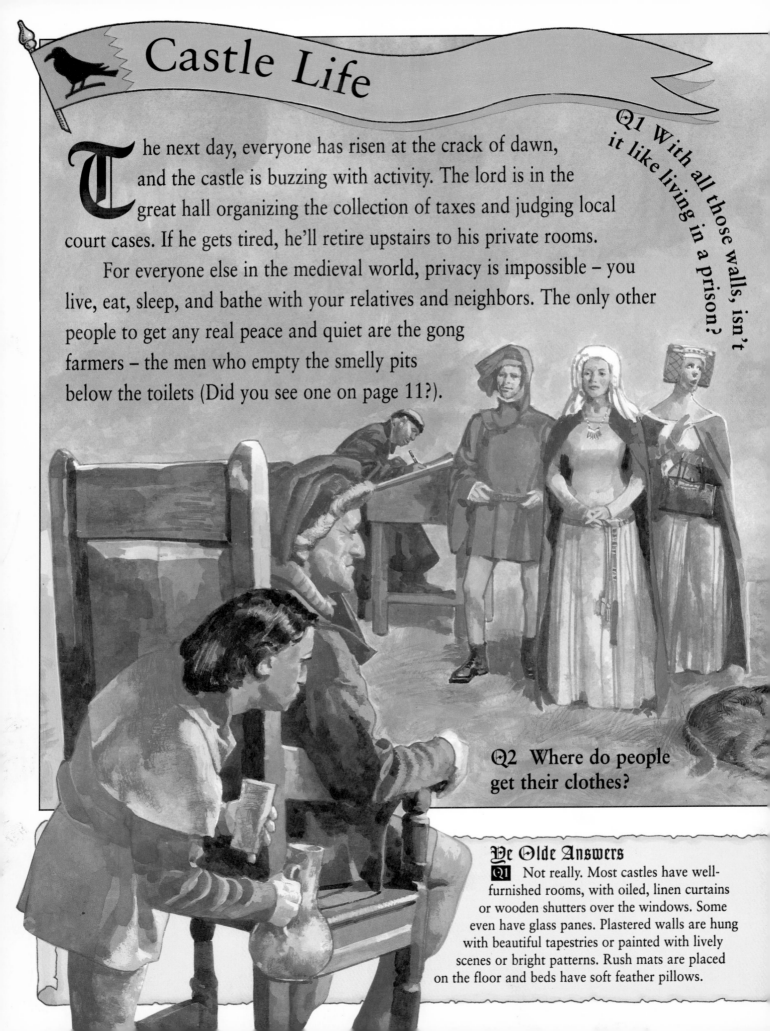

The next day, everyone has risen at the crack of dawn, and the castle is buzzing with activity. The lord is in the great hall organizing the collection of taxes and judging local court cases. If he gets tired, he'll retire upstairs to his private rooms.

For everyone else in the medieval world, privacy is impossible – you live, eat, sleep, and bathe with your relatives and neighbors. The only other people to get any real peace and quiet are the gong farmers – the men who empty the smelly pits below the toilets (Did you see one on page 11?).

Q1 With all those walls, isn't it like living in a prison?

Q2 Where do people get their clothes?

Ye Olde Answers

Q1 Not really. Most castles have well-furnished rooms, with oiled, linen curtains or wooden shutters over the windows. Some even have glass panes. Plastered walls are hung with beautiful tapestries or painted with lively scenes or bright patterns. Rush mats are placed on the floor and beds have soft feather pillows.

Jester's Quest
Can you spot the handbag, boots, fountain pen, and tie? Which don't belong in a medieval castle?

Q3 What is life like for women?

True or False?
Medieval men only wore clothes they could fight in.

Castle Life Puzzle

1. As most nobles own several castles and regularly move from one to the next, their furniture can be separated into smaller parts and put together again. What piece of furniture do you think is made from these parts (*above*)?

2. **a** Who has a haircut like this?

b Who would use this tool?

c Who would wear a hat like this?

Q2 There are no stores, so rich people pay tailors to make their clothes. Fashions in hats, shoes, hairstyles, dresses, and coats vary from year to year. In some countries, the law allows only the rich to wear fine clothes. In others, trendy fashions are banned!

Q3 Boring if you are rich, and hard work if you are poor. Most women are valued only as mothers and have few rights or possessions. Other than personal servants, the only working women in the castle are laundresses, though the lady is in charge of the castle when the lord is away.

Castle Life Puzzle
1. It's a four-poster bed, one of a lord's favorite possessions!
2. a priest. b blacksmith. c beekeeper.

Jester's Quest: None of them! For the reasons why, see page 28.

Priests and Prayers

Q1 What does the priest do?

Hunt the Assassin

What is the most important subject taught to medieval children?

a Manners = Green tunic
b Fighting = Yellow tunic
c Dancing = Blue tunic

Use your clue to uncover the assassin on p. 29.

Education Puzzle

Noble children are taught by their mother or a priest. As they have to live their lives according to set rules, the most important subject is manners. Which of these subjects do you think girls are taught, and which subjects boys?

- Latin • Dancing
- Chemistry
- Medicine • Math
- Riding & hunting
- Weaving, spinning, and needlework

Ye Olde Answers

Q1 As well as his religious duties in the chapel, the castle priest is often put in charge of castle documents as he is one of the few people in a castle who can read or write. In large castles a priest has several clerks to help him. A few priests even act as spies for their lord. No one questions their comings and goings, and their robe acts as a perfect disguise.

Furthermore, their knowledge of writing proves a valuable spying weapon!

The castle day begins in the chapel. With its painted walls, stained-glass windows, and golden objects, this is the most beautiful room in the castle. The service is being performed by a priest, who also says grace before meals.

Medieval people believe that they can't get through life without help from God or magical forces, so most obey the Church's strict rules about how to lead their lives. For example, Christians are told not to eat meat on Wednesdays, Fridays, Saturdays or Holy Days, so most castles have fish ponds, allowing the lord to eat fish instead.

Q2 How important is the Church?

Because printing hasn't been invented (and won't be until the mid-15th century), all books are copied by hand and written on parchment, usually by monks. The parchment is made from goatskins or sheepskins. The skins are softened in urine, the hairs are scraped off, and then they are stretched and polished.

A Mysterious Manuscript

Books often have beautiful pictures and symbols next to the writing. Like the sculptures and paintings on the wall of the chapel, these teach people who can't read the words of God.

Some of the monks add extra little details and pictures, just for fun. Look at the picture (*right*) and see if you can find the face of the monk that drew it.

True or False? Some priests never talked to each other.

Q2 Very. The rich give treasures and money to the Church as thanks for blessings from God and to show their wealth. Poor people must pay taxes (called a tithe) to the Church. The Church plays a very important part in politics as well – many bishops even own their castles.

Education Puzzle

• Latin – *Girls and boys, as Latin is the language spoken by all educated people in Europe.* • Dancing – *Girls and boys, as it is an important part of a nobles' social life.* • Chemistry – *There isn't much scientific learning,* but a few boys are taught by magical scientists called alchemists.* • Medicine – *Girls are taught herbal cures and how to dress wounds.* • Math – *Girls, to do the castle accounts.* • Riding & hunting – *Boys and girls.* • Weaving etc. – *Girls learn how to spin wool, weave cloth, and sew.*

From Page to Knight

Out in the yard, young lads are training to become knights. The boys will have left home at seven to begin their training. They are called pages first and then esquires at the age of 14. It's a hard life, but worth it. When they have become knights the lord will depend on them for his power. Knights are the most important fighting men in the Medieval world, and in return for their support the lord will give them some of his land.

The boys aren't just learning how to fight – there are many other jobs around the castle that they must do. They will also learn about chivalry, the knight's code. Knights are expected to be honorable and brave, to protect the weak, and to respect women.

Medieval Maze

Can the young lady at the bottom of the maze reach her lover in the center without bumping into her guardian?

Q1 Do monks ever fight?

Medieval Maze

Marriages between nobles are arranged while the children are still very young. But young men and women still enjoy spending their time listening to songs and reading poems about love. A favorite place for this is the pleasure garden with flowers and fountains, called "Gardens of Love," mazes are a particularly good place for courting!

Pages Puzzle

What jobs can you see pages and esquires doing around the castle?

esquire

page

Q1 Yes. In addition to the legendary Friar Tuck, there are knights who are monks. The Knights Hospitaller were formed to look after the sick, and the Knights Templar to protect pilgrims going to the Holy Land. Both fought in the Crusades (a holy war to capture Jerusalem from the Muslims).

Pages Puzzle

In the keep, pages (P) and esquires (E) are: • dressing the lord (E) • bringing water for washing (P) • praying for guidance on how to be a good knight (E) • sweeping the floor (P) • carving the meat (P) • serving at the table (P) • helping in the kitchens (P).

In the courtyard they are: • learning to fight with wooden swords (P), maces (clubs), and shields (E) • learning archery (P) • learning (P) and teaching (E) riding • practicing jousting (P). In the stables they are: • looking after the horses (E) • cleaning the armor (E) • sharpening swords (E).

Like the pages on page 16, these knights are training for battle. The two here are jousting, and one has just been knocked off his horse by his opponent, who is the winner. The joust has special rules, and takes place in an area known as the lists, where the knights are separated by a barrier called the tilt.

Knocking an opponent over is just one way of winning. Knights also score points (and earn money) by breaking their lance on an opponent's shield.

True or False?
Knights used only one lance in a tournament.

Jester's Quest
Can you spot the scarves, eyeglasses, umbrella, beer bottle, and Band-Aid? Which don't belong in a medieval joust?

Q1 Isn't jousting a little dangerous?

Q2 Does anyone cheat?

Ye Olde Answers

Q1 It certainly is! Pope Innocent III even banned jousting because it was so dangerous. Knights wear extra thick armor but many are still injured or killed. Jousting lances are blunted, but they become lethal weapons if they split or hit someone in the throat.

Q2 Some knights do, especially in a team game called a *tourney* (see page 21). This is like a real battle – there are few rules and fighting lasts all day. Knights cheat by pretending not to compete then joining in toward the end. By this time, their opponents are tired, so it is easy to win.

Armor Puzzle
The pieces are: *a* – Spurs *b* – Knee-piece *c* – Greave *d* – Sabaton *e* – Pauldron *f* – Gauntlet.

Jesters Quest: Umbrellas, sticky plasters and beer bottles don't belong in a joust. Full answers on page 28.

Hunt the Assassin

How much does a suit of armor weigh?

a 50 pounds = Blue leggings
b 80 pounds = Red leggings
c 100 pounds = Green leggings

Use your answer to uncover the assassin on page 29.

Q3 What is it like wearing armor?

Q3 Armor looks uncomfortable, but is actually quite easy to move around in. It usually weighs about 45-55 lbs. But what if a knight wants to relieve himself? In battle he'd be too excited or busy to think about it. At other times he might lift up his chain-mail coat, then open his codpiece, a special flap of clothing on the front of his woolen leggings. However, no one knows for sure!

Armor Puzzle

Early knights were protected by a coat of chain mail (a long shirt of iron rings linked together). By 1350, solid plates of steel were added to protect the legs, arms, and chest. Each piece of armor has a special name (*below*).

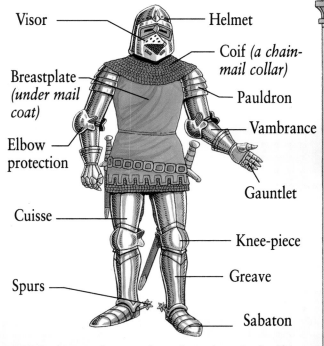

Visor — Helmet

Coif (*a chain-mail collar*)

Breastplate (*under mail coat*)

Pauldron

Vambrance

Elbow protection

Gauntlet

Cuisse

Knee-piece

Greave

Spurs

Sabaton

Which pieces of armor have been knocked off in the fight below? (See panel below for answer.)

a
b
c
d
e
f

19

Heraldry

The Family Coat of Arms

This family tree shows how a coat of arms (the family "badge") is passed down from one generation to the next. Daughters are shown by diamond shapes and sons by shields.

Heir   Eleanor   John   Non-heiress   Richard   Heiress   Stephen

New family coat of arms is formed.

New family coat of arms is formed.

New family coat of arms is formed.

William

Henry   Matilda   Guy

Edward   Mary

🃏 **Jester's Quest**
Can you spot the boxing gloves, spurs, sandwich, and sling? Which don't belong in a medieval tournament?

Oldest sons are shown by a bar 🔲, 2nd sons by a crescent ☽, 3rd sons by a mullet ★, and so on.

Q1 What are heralds?

Heraldry Explained

The family tree shows how medieval men think that they are all-important. Fathers always get to pass their arms onto their children, but mothers only did if they had no brothers. For example, after Eleanor marries, her arms are placed next to her husband's to form a new coat of arms. Her brothers John and Richard also combine their arms with their wives. But as Richard's wife is an heiress (i.e. she has no brothers), her arms are placed inside his. In the next generation, Henry, Matilda, and Guy combine their parents' arms in quarters, because their mother is an heiress. Meanwhile, William, Edward, and Mary use only their father's arms, as their mothers are not heiresses.

Jesters Quest: Sandwiches, boxing gloves and slings don't belong. For the reasons why, turn to page 28.

These knights are taking part in a mock battle, called a tourney. But how can they tell friend from foe when everyone is covered from head to toe in armor? – by looking at the badge with which every knight decorates his shield and tunic. This system, called heraldry, meant you could tell from which family a knight came, to whom he was married and even if he had an older brother!

Heraldry Puzzle

If you look at the family tree on page 20 you will see how a family coat of arms is altered for different members of the family. Using what you have learned, can you figure out which two other knights are related to the Sir Loins in the main picture.

Sir Loins

Q1 Heralds are the men who design coats of arms and make sure that no two designs are the same. They also announce knights at tournaments. After a battle, they have the rather horrible job of figuring out who the dead or dying knights are from their coats of arms.

Heraldry Puzzle

Sir Loins (a) is related to Sir Gerry (b) and Sir Vice (c). You can tell because both Sir Loins and Sir Vice have a wavy yellow stripe on a green background in their coat of arms. Both Sir Loins and Sir Gerry have a white cross on a black background (*right*).

There isn't enough land inside the castle walls to grow crops or keep animals, so food for the castle comes from the fields outside.

Most of the land surrounding the castle is owned by the lord, and he makes the peasants living on the land work for him one day out of every four. In return, he gives them small

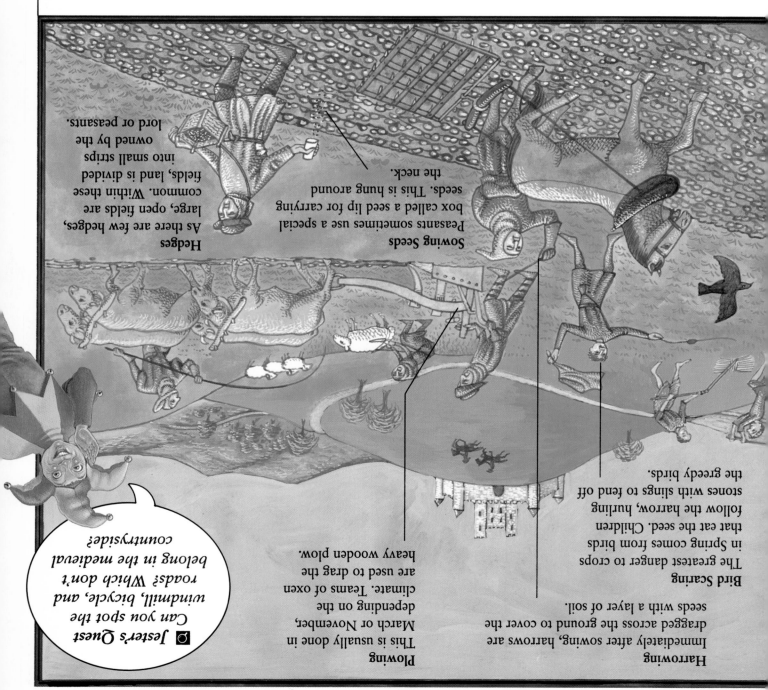

Hedges
As there are few hedges, large, open fields are common. Within these fields, land is divided into small strips owned by the lord or peasants.

Sowing Seeds
Peasants sometimes use a special box called a seed lip for carrying seeds. This is hung around the neck.

Bird Scaring
The greatest danger to crops in spring comes from birds that eat the seed. Children follow the harrow, hurling stones with slings to fend off the greedy birds.

Harrowing
Immediately after sowing, harrows are dragged across the ground to cover the seeds with a layer of soil.

Plowing
This is usually done in March or November, depending on the climate. Teams of oxen are used to drag the heavy wooden plow.

Jester's Quest
Can you spot the windmill, bicycle, and roads? Which don't belong in the medieval countryside?

Country Puzzle
Can you guess what all these people are up to and what they use these objects for? For the answer, turn the book upside down.

plots of land to farm for themselves. The farmers grow peas and beans to dry for the winter and grains like wheat, barley and oats.

◎ *Jesters Quest: bicycles and roads don't belong. For the reasons why, turn to page 29.*

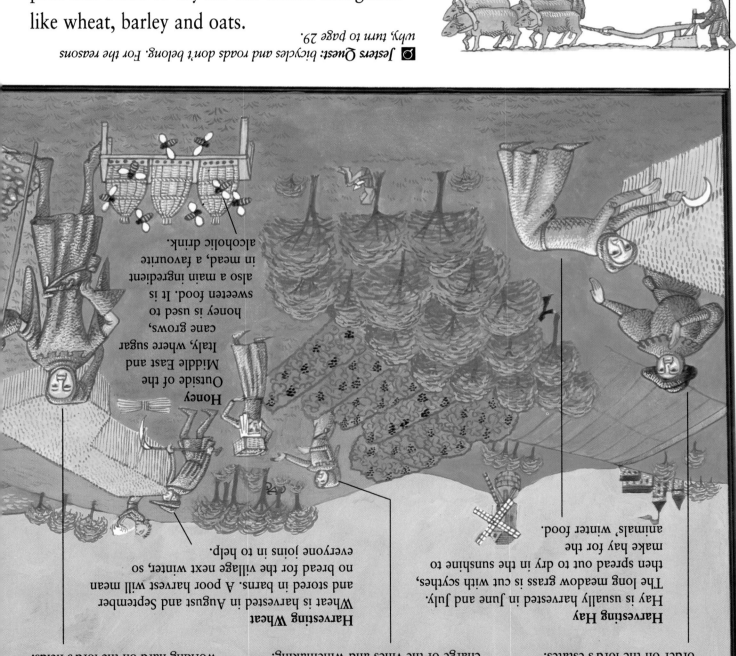

Honey
Outside of the Middle East and Italy, where sugar cane grows, honey is used to sweeten food. It is also a main ingredient in mead, a favourite alcoholic drink.

Harvesting Wheat
Wheat is harvested in August and September and stored in barns. A poor harvest will mean no bread for the village next winter, so everyone joins in to help.

Harvesting Hay
Hay is usually harvested in June and July. The long meadow grass is cut with scythes, then spread out to dry in the sunshine to make hay for the animals' winter food.

Bailiff
The bailiff is employed by the lord to help run the estate. He makes sure the peasants are working hard on the lord's fields.

Butler
The bottler, or 'butler', looks after the castle's supplies of wine. In grape-growing regions, he is also in charge of the vines and winemaking.

Reeve
The Shire Reeve (which later became 'Sheriff' in English) is responsible for law and order on the lord's estates.

Out Hunting

Hunting is an important source of meat for the lord's table, and is good training for war. It is also the favorite sport of most lords and ladies, and many of them keep special horses just for this.

Hunting dogs are used to sniff out animals and track them down. Some wear special collars to protect their throats, in case a wild boar tries to gore them with its sharp tusks.

The dogs are better cared for than the servants that look after them. Living in heated kennels, the dogs even have special bread, called brom bread, baked for their dinner.

Ye Olde Answers

Q1 Throughout medieval times, large areas of European forests have been cleared and turned into farmland. But special areas of woodland have been set aside for hunting deer, wild boars, foxes, and bears. However, only nobles are allowed to hunt and fish in these areas. Any peasants caught poaching animals might be blinded or killed, though many still try to catch a squirrel or rabbit for dinner.

Q2 The bird you hunt with depends on how important you are. For example, an emperor hunted with an eagle, a king or queen with a gyrfalcon, a lord with a peregrine falcon, and a noblewoman with a hawk. The trained birds live like kings – perched on their owners' wrists, they travel everywhere with them, even to meals and church!

True or False?
Pigs were trained by poachers to help them hunt.

🔍 **Jester's Quest**
Can you spot the chariot, hunting horn, shotgun, and binoculars? Which don't belong in a medieval hunt?

Q1 Who is allowed to hunt?

Q2 What birds are used for hunting?

Hunting Puzzle

1 The birds of prey used to catch other animals were trained with special equipment. Can you guess how a, b, c, and d were used?

a b c d

2 Seven animals are hiding or running from the hunters in the main scene. What are they?

🦅 Hunting Puzzle

1a Glove (to protect a trainer's arm from being scratched by the bird's sharp claws). b Bells (to let you know where the hawk is). c Hood (to keep the bird calm when it is not hunting). d Leash (to stop the bird from flying away until the right moment).
2 The hunted animals are (from left to right): wild boars, stork, rabbit, bear, wolf, deer, and fox. And no, the assassin doesn't count!

🔍 Jester's Quest: Chariot, shotgun, and binoculars don't belong. For reasons why see page 29.

Under Siege!

While the lord was out hunting, his rival surrounded the castle (Did you see the enemy army on page 25?). After burning down the homes of local people, the enemy lord normally just waits for the people inside the castle to starve. But, as fresh weapons and supplies appear to be getting inside, he has decided to attack.

Siege weapons are hurling great boulders and flaming arrows at the walls while mighty siege towers are being pulled toward the walls, to allow soldiers to jump onto the castle ramparts. The defenders are sheltering behind the walls and shooting arrows at the attackers.

Q1 How do you get in?

Q2 Are there lots of tunnels under the walls?

Ye Olde Answers

Q1 It really depends on how desperate you are to get in. If you have time, the best way is to starve out the castle or poison the water supply. If you are in more of a hurry, then you try a combination of:
• Setting the castle on fire with flaming arrows • Digging a tunnel below the walls to bring them down • Knocking holes in the walls with stone throwers (called trebuchets) • Battering the gate down with a ram (one is attacking the gatehouse on page 30) • Storming the walls with ladders and siege towers.

Q2 During a siege, yes! Once a moat has been drained or filled in (as in the main picture) the attackers dig their way under the castle walls. They then light a fire in the tunnel so the timbers holding up the roof of the tunnel collapse. This makes the walls above tumble down. ☞

Hunt the Assassin

What was the castle moat for:

a Swimming in = Short person

b To make it hard to attack the castle = Tall person

c To keep fish in = Average

Now you have all six clues, try to spot the assassin on page 29.

Q3 Can you cheat at sieging?

Jester's Quest
Try to spot the musket, telescope, dead cow, samurai, and parachute? Which don't belong in a siege?

Some castles have a Sally Port. This secret tunnel allows the defenders to sneak fresh supplies and troops into the castle. When Heddingham Castle in England was being besieged, the defenders cheekily chucked fresh fish at their attackers to show they would never be starved into surrender!

Q3 Of course! In 1312, Linlithgow Castle was captured by men hiding in a cart of hay. Many others were captured by treachery. In 1306, for example, the English Prince Edward bribed the blacksmith of Kildrummy Castle to set fire to the castle stores. The castle soon surrendered (though the blacksmith was rewarded with molten metal being poured down his throat!).

Jester's Quest: The samurai, telescope, and parachute don't belong. For the reasons why see page 29.

Jester's Quest

Pages 4–5

Glass was first made in 1500 B.C, but *windows* were a luxury. If a castle had any, they would be in the chapel. Even if you had a *television* (it wasn't invented until 1928) you couldn't have watched it – no homes had electricity until the late 19th century! *Pipe*-smoking (*top*) was also out until tobacco was brought back from America after its discovery in 1492. *Hammers* have been used since ancient times.

Pages 6-7

Medieval Europeans knew little of the world beyond North Africa and the Middle East (*above*), so American foods like *potatoes, corn,* and *pineapples* were unknown. Likewise, tropical *bananas* were not known and *tea* from India/China did not reach Europe until 1610. *Beer* had been known since 4000 B.C. A ground-meat dish, like a *burger,* was eaten and medieval cooks knew how to make *jelly.*

Pages 8–9

Though monks invented a form of *tennis* in the 13th century, modern lawn tennis was introduced in 1873. A far more common sight was a game of football (*right*) played by mobs in the streets! *Guitars* weren't made until the 18th century, but lutes (big mandolins with 11 strings) were a common sight (see page 7). *Walkmans* are a modern invention, while *watches* with springs weren't made until the 16th century.

Pages 10-11

The Egyptian *mummy's coffin* had been around for thousands of years, but you wouldn't expect to find one in a European medieval castle! *Torture racks* were a favorite medieval torture instrument (but not with prisoners)! A few castle rooms had *running water*, but it only came in two temperatures – cold and freezing! *Telephones* were invented in 1876, but if you wanted to send a message in the Middle Ages, it was either delivered by a mounted courier (*above*), or by a homing pigeon (the assassin is using one on page 17).

Pages 12–13

Pens made from feathers (called quills, *left*) had been in use since 500 B.C., but fountain pens were only invented in the 19th century. There were no *handbags* in the medieval world. But when women went to town they did carry a small bag filled with sweet-smelling herbs – to cover up the awful smell of the streets. There weren't really any medieval *boots*. Most medieval shoes were more like slippers though some had wooden platforms

for walking through the mud. Also, there were no laces to tie up at the front until the 17th century. The first *ties* were cravats worn in the early 17th century. But some ties do work just like medieval heraldry – their colors tell you what school or club someone belongs to.

Pages 18–19

The first known *eyeglasses* appear in a French manuscript of the 14th century. There weren't football *scarves,* but ladies did tie their scarf to a knight to show they favored him. Beer was usually served from jugs. It was only put into *bottles* in the 17th century. *Umbrellas* were used by the ancient Egyptians as sunshades, but they were only widely used against rain in the 1700s. *Band-Aids* are a 20th century invention. Medieval doctors sometimes used bleeding as a cure, using leeches to suck out "bad" blood.

Pages 20–21

Boxing gloves weren't used until the

Hunt the Assassin
Did you see the assassin's clothes on pages 5, 13, 16, 19, 22, 24, & 26? Use what you've seen with the clues from pages 5, 6, 10, 14, 19, and 27 to figure out who he is in the lineup on the right. If you can't tell who it is, some of your answers must be wrong!

end of the 19th century – but then you'd hardly use a boxing glove if you had a sword! **Spurs** were used by medieval knights to control the movement of their horse. People had eaten food with bread since ancient times, but the word **sandwich** comes from an English lord of the 1700s who ate sandwiches while he played cards. The **sling** was a dangerous weapon in ancient times, but was gradually replaced by the bow and arrow.

Pages 22–23

The first **bicycle**, a wooden scooterlike vehicle, was invented in about 1790. Invented in Iran in the 7th century, **windmills** spread to Europe by 1100, where they soon dotted the landscape. Most medieval **roads** were little more than a clear path through the forest, though some stone roads survived from the days of Roman road builders (*right*).

Pages 24–25

There were no medieval **shotguns** – like Robin Hood, hunters used a bow and arrow. **Binoculars** were a 19th-century invention. In ancient times, **chariots** were a battle winner, but the invention of the stirrup and

saddle by 500 A.D. meant that men fought from horseback not chariots. **Hunting horns** had been in use since prehistoric times.

Page 26–27

14th-century **samurai**s were like knights – they wore plate armor, fought in a similar way, and followed a code of honor – but it is unlikely any would have made their way from Japan to Europe! There wasn't much need for **parachutes** until the invention of airplanes, but in the medieval world you might have seen tower jumpers – crazy daredevils who strapped wings to themselves and tried to fly off tall buildings (*left*)! The first **muskets** (*right*) date from 1388 and were handheld cannons that were almost as dangerous to the firer as the target! **Dead cows** were catapulted onto the walls in an attempt to spread disease among the inhabitants of the castle. **Telescopes** were only invented later, in 1608, by Dutchman Hans Lippershey.

True or False

Page 5 True – In 1139, Henry of Bourboug got his architects to measure

the site of a ruined castle close to the center of a rebellion. They then made wooden sections which, together, would form a whole castle. The rebels got a nasty shock the next day!

Page 9 True – Troubadours were welcome in any castle, so they were well placed to get information about rivals.

Page 10 True – Some drawbridges were designed with trapdoors to drop unwanted visitors into a pit.

Page 13 False – Some men's shoes were so pointed that the toes had to be tied back – not very practical for fighting!

Page 15 True – Priests were divided into groups, called orders. Each order had its own rules, and some asked their priests to take a vow of silence. To talk, they used sign language, hissed, or pulled faces at each other!

Page 18 False – Crowds loved the sound of splintering lances. One knight broke over 300 lances in a day.

Page 25 True – Poachers did use pigs' great sense of smell to track down prey.

> AND FINALLY…
> See if you can escape the assassin in the exciting castle game – just turn over the page!

John Whistlegrub   Sir Roger de Courcey   Geoffrey Tuck   Little Dick   Simon de Vile   Will Fletcher   Much Tyler   Stephen Tadger   Bob Tanner

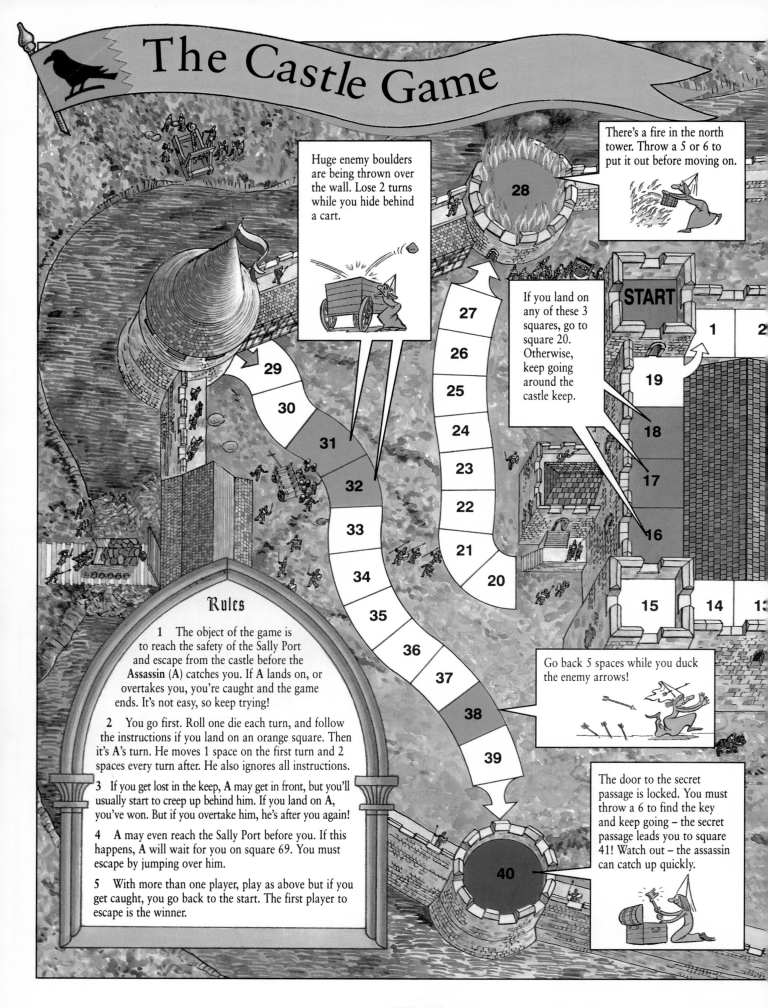

The Castle Game

Huge enemy boulders are being thrown over the wall. Lose 2 turns while you hide behind a cart.

There's a fire in the north tower. Throw a 5 or 6 to put it out before moving on.

START

If you land on any of these 3 squares, go to square 20. Otherwise, keep going around the castle keep.

28

27
26
25
24
23
22
21
20

29
30
31
32
33
34
35
36
37
38
39

19
18
17
16
15
14
13
1
2

40

Go back 5 spaces while you duck the enemy arrows!

The door to the secret passage is locked. You must throw a 6 to find the key and keep going – the secret passage leads you to square 41! Watch out – the assassin can catch up quickly.

Rules

1 The object of the game is to reach the safety of the Sally Port and escape from the castle before the **Assassin (A)** catches you. If A lands on, or overtakes you, you're caught and the game ends. It's not easy, so keep trying!

2 You go first. Roll one die each turn, and follow the instructions if you land on an orange square. Then it's A's turn. He moves 1 space on the first turn and 2 spaces every turn after. He also ignores all instructions.

3 If you get lost in the keep, A may get in front, but you'll usually start to creep up behind him. If you land on A, you've won. But if you overtake him, he's after you again!

4 A may even reach the Sally Port before you. If this happens, A will wait for you on square 69. You must escape by jumping over him.

5 With more than one player, play as above but if you get caught, you go back to the start. The first player to escape is the winner.

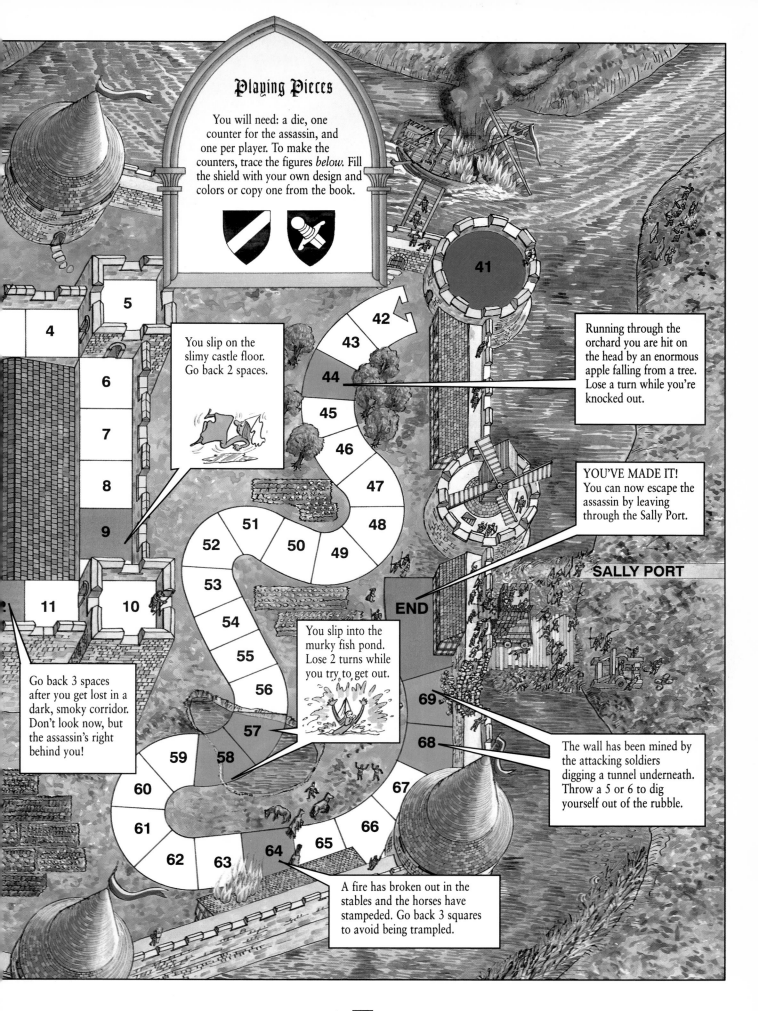

Playing Pieces

You will need: a die, one counter for the assassin, and one per player. To make the counters, trace the figures *below*. Fill the shield with your own design and colors or copy one from the book.

4

5

6

7

8

9

10

11

You slip on the slimy castle floor. Go back 2 spaces.

Go back 3 spaces after you get lost in a dark, smoky corridor. Don't look now, but the assassin's right behind you!

41

42

43

44

45

46

47

48

49

50

51

52

53

54

55

56

57

58

59

60

61

62

63

64

65

66

67

68

69

END

Running through the orchard you are hit on the head by an enormous apple falling from a tree. Lose a turn while you're knocked out.

YOU'VE MADE IT! You can now escape the assassin by leaving through the Sally Port.

SALLY PORT

You slip into the murky fish pond. Lose 2 turns while you try to get out.

The wall has been mined by the attacking soldiers digging a tunnel underneath. Throw a 5 or 6 to dig yourself out of the rubble.

A fire has broken out in the stables and the horses have stampeded. Go back 3 squares to avoid being trampled.

The Index

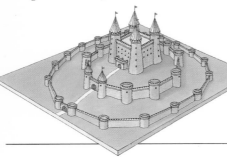

The Assassin Unmasked!

Gotcha! All along it was that knave Simon de Vile (left) lurking beneath the cloak. Did you identify him? Turn to page 11 and you can even catch the villain in the act as he pours a deadly poison into the queen's dish.

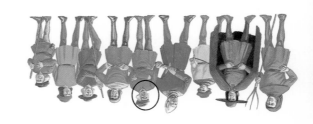